P9-ARM-356

3 1526 03413120 8

The Largest Planet

Jupiter

by Nancy Loewen   illustrated by Jeff Yesh

PICTURE WINDOW BOOKS
Minneapolis, Minnesota

HARFORD COUNTY
PUBLIC LIBRARY
100 E. Pennsylvania Avenue
Bel Air, MD 21014

Thanks to our advisers for their expertise, research, and advice:

Lynne Hillenbrand, Ph.D., Professor of Astronomy
California Institute of Technology

Terry Flaherty, Ph.D., Professor of English
Minnesota State University, Mankato

Editor: Jill Kalz
Designers: Amy Muehlenhardt and Melissa Kes
Page Production: Melissa Kes
Art Director: Nathan Gassman
Associate Managing Editor: Christianne Jones
The illustrations in this book were created digitally.

Picture Window Books
5115 Excelsior Boulevard
Suite 232
Minneapolis, MN 55416
877-845-8392
www.picturewindowbooks.com

Copyright © 2008 by Picture Window Books
All rights reserved. No part of this book may
be reproduced without written permission from
the publisher. The publisher takes no responsibility
for the use of any of the materials or methods
described in this book, nor for the products thereof.

Printed in the United States of America.

 All books published by Picture Window Books
are manufactured with paper containing at least
10 percent post-consumer waste.

Library of Congress Cataloging-in-Publication Data
Loewen, Nancy, 1964-
The largest planet : Jupiter / by Nancy Loewen ; illustrated by Jeff Yesh.
p. cm. — (Amazing science. Planets)
Includes index.
ISBN: 978-1-4048-3952-6 (library binding)
ISBN: 978-1-4048-3961-8 (paperback)
1. Jupiter (Planet)—Juvenile literature. I. Yesh, Jeff, 1971- ill. II. Title.
QB661.L64 2008
523.45—dc22   2007032886

Table of Contents

Think Big

Think of something that's big. Really, really big.

What did you think of? A skyscraper? A mountain? An ocean?
Maybe you thought of the planet Earth.

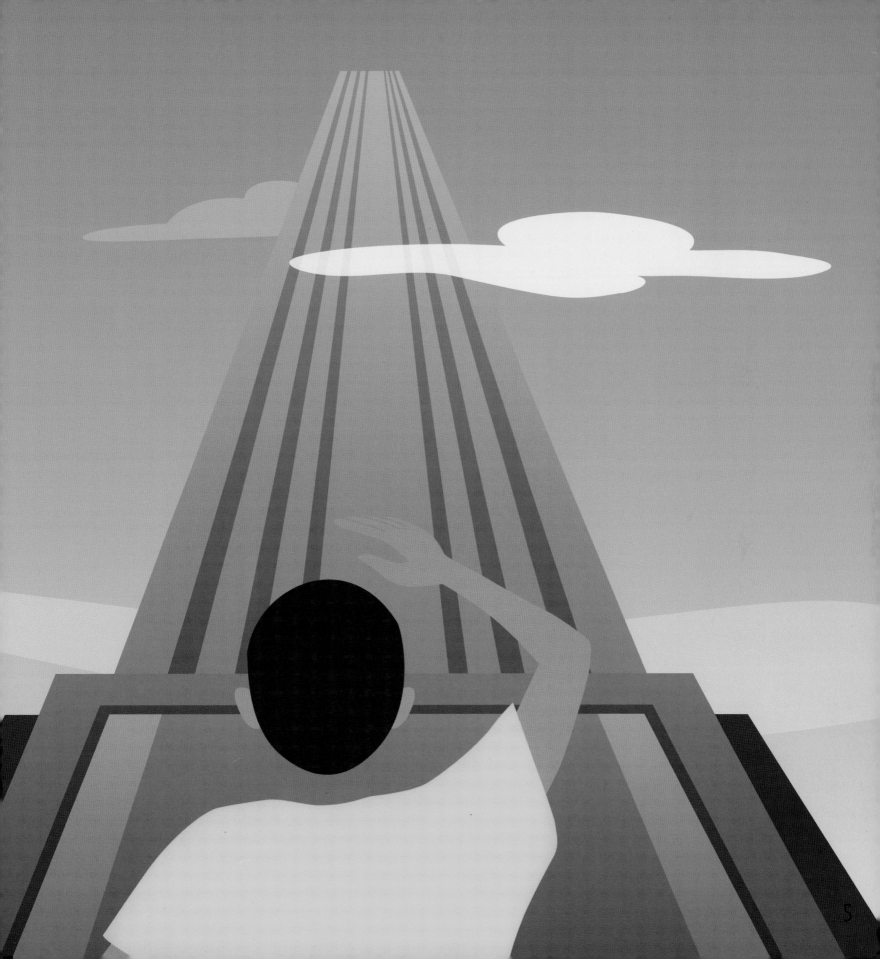

King of the Planets

Earth seems huge to us. But it's actually one of the smaller planets in our solar system. Jupiter is the largest. It was named after the king of the Roman gods.

6

Jupiter's diameter = 88,700 miles (141,920 kilometers)

Jupiter

Mercury

Venus

Earth

Mars

Uranus

Saturn

Neptune

FUN FACT
Jupiter's diameter is more than 11 times greater
than Earth's.

One of the Brightest

Not only is Jupiter big, but it's also very bright. It is one of the brightest objects in the sky. Only the sun, moon, and the planet Venus are brighter.

Many of the other planets can't be seen easily with the naked eye, but Jupiter can. Even ancient people knew about Jupiter. They called it the "Wandering Star."

Jupiter

Uranus

Neptune

Saturn

Mercury

Venus

Earth

Mars

FUN FACT

Of our solar system's eight planets—Mercury,
Venus, Earth, Mars, Jupiter, Saturn, Uranus, and
Neptune—Jupiter is the fifth planet from the sun.
Its nearest neighbors are Mars and Saturn.

EDITOR'S NOTE

In this illustration, the distances between planets
are not to scale. In reality, the distances between
the outer planets are much greater than the
distances between the inner planets.

Super Spin

Jupiter is big, but it's not slow. The planet spins, or rotates, on its axis faster than any other planet. A full turn is one day. Every 10 Earth hours, Jupiter completes a full turn. On Earth, a full turn takes 24 hours.

Jupiter is much farther away from the sun than Earth is. As a result, its year is much longer. Jupiter takes almost 12 Earth years to complete its orbit around the sun.

FUN FACT
The area between the orbits of Mars and Jupiter is called the asteroid belt. It is filled with tens of thousands of asteroids. Asteroids are rocks that orbit around the sun. Some may measure more than 500 miles (800 km) across!

Under Pressure

People usually think of planets as being solid balls of rock. But Jupiter doesn't have a solid surface. It is made mostly of gas. The gas is mostly hydrogen, mixed with some helium.

Under great pressure, the hydrogen gets more tightly packed the closer it gets to the center, or core, of the planet. The gas gets so dense at the core that it turns into a metallic liquid.

FUN FACT

Because Jupiter is made mostly of gas, it's called a gas giant planet. The other gas giants are Saturn, Uranus, and Neptune. Mercury, Venus, Mars, and Earth are terrestrial, or rocky, planets.

13

Zones and Belts

Viewed through a telescope, Jupiter looks like a beautiful marble. Bands of reddish-brown, bluish-white, and orange swirl around it.

These bands of color are clouds of gas. Strong winds sweep the clouds around the planet. Some bands move in an east-to-west direction. Others move in a west-to-east direction. Areas with thinner clouds appear bluish.

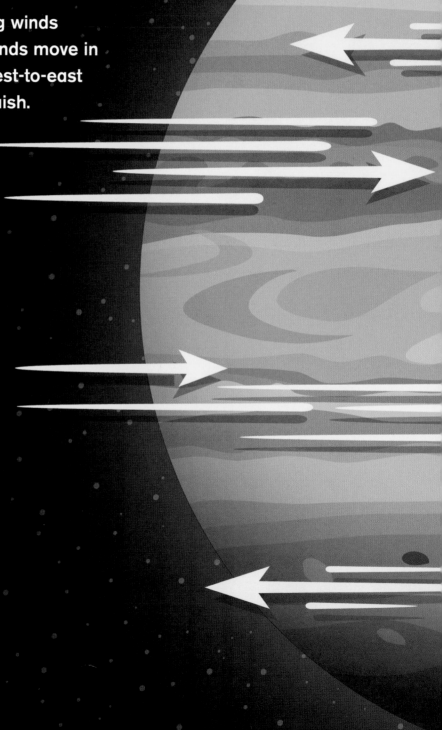

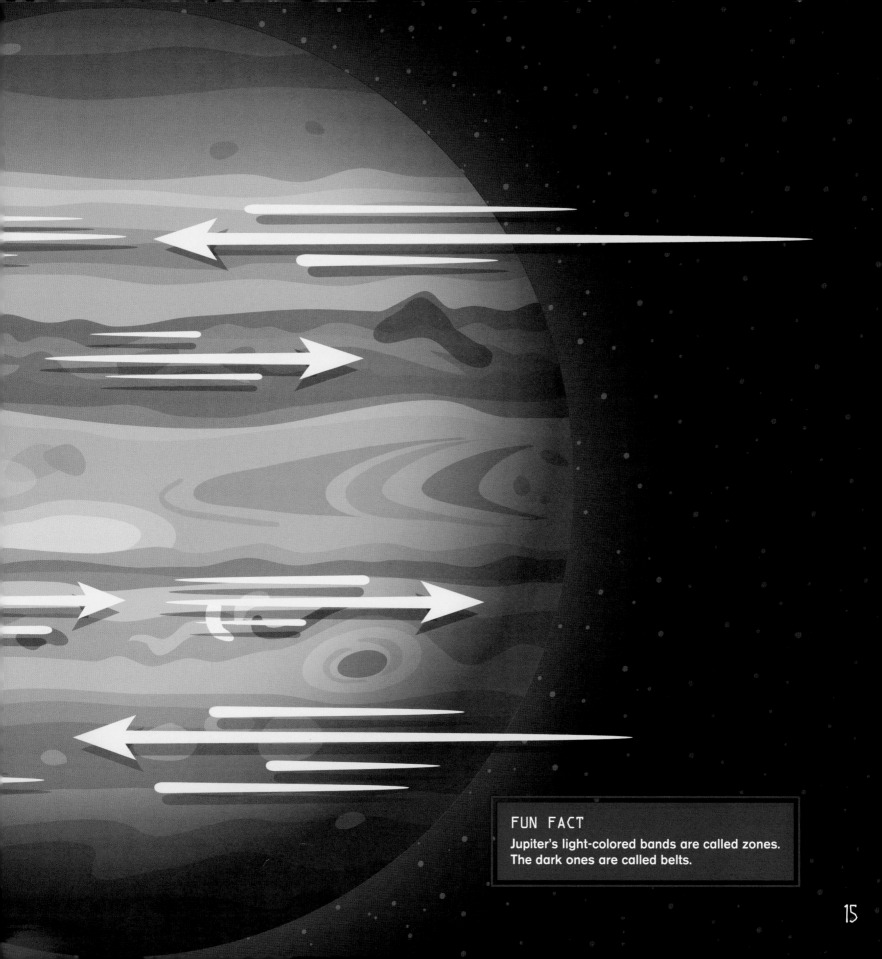

FUN FACT
Jupiter's light-colored bands are called zones.
The dark ones are called belts.

The Great Red Spot

On Jupiter's southern half lies something that looks like a big freckle. This reddish-brown spot is a huge, hurricane-like storm. It has been raging for hundreds of years. The Great Red Spot is the largest storm in the solar system. It is twice as wide as Earth!

A similar storm is growing nearby. Scientists first saw the new spot in the year 2000.

The Great Red Spot

FUN FACT
Like Saturn, Jupiter has rings. *Voyager 1* discovered them in 1979. The three faint rings are made of bits of rocky material and dust.

Moon Magnet

Jupiter has the strongest gravity of any planet in our solar system. Its gravity is about 2.5 times stronger than Earth's.

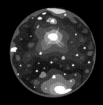

Jupiter pulls other objects toward it, just like Earth pulls the moon. But while the Earth has just one moon, Jupiter has four large ones and nearly 60 small ones—and maybe more!

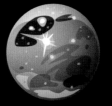

FUN FACT

Jupiter's gravity is very strong. A person weighing 100 pounds (45 kilograms) on Earth would weigh about 240 pounds (108 kg) on Jupiter.

19

The Galilean Moons

The Italian scientist Galileo Galilei discovered Jupiter's four largest moons in 1610 with one of the very first telescopes. The moons are Io, Callisto, Europa, and Ganymede. Because Galilei found them, they are known as the Galilean moons.

Scientists hope that studying Jupiter and its moons will help us learn more about how our solar system was formed.

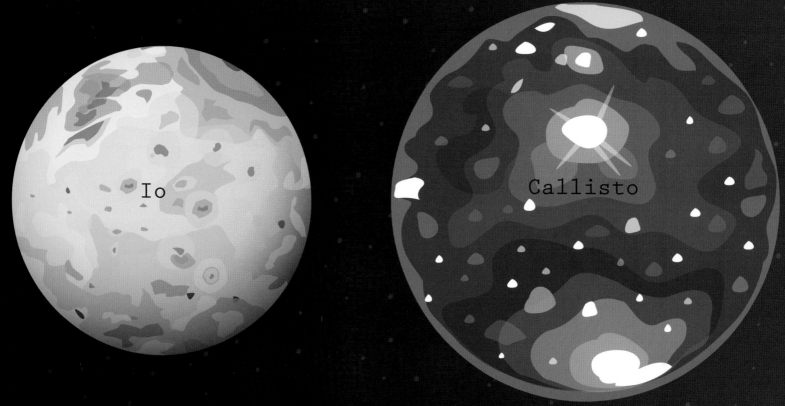

Io

Callisto

Europa

Ganymede

FUN FACT
The moon Io has more active volcanoes than any object in our solar system.

Planets Big and Small

What you need:

- a piece of paper
- a ruler
- a pencil
- colored pencils in eight different colors

What you do:

1. Using the pencil and ruler, make a big plus sign (+) on the piece of paper. Both lines should be 7 inches (17.8 centimeters) long. The lines should cross exactly in the middle.

2. With a colored pencil, draw a circle around the outside edges of the plus sign. Label this circle "Jupiter."

3. Now measure 3 inches (7.6 cm) from the center of the plus sign. Make a dot on each of the four lines. Using a different colored pencil, draw a circle to connect them. Label this circle "Saturn."

4. Continue making circles using the following measurements and label them. All measurements are from the center of the plus sign.

2.5 inches (6.4 cm) Uranus	.5 inches (1.3 cm) Venus
Slightly less than 2.5 inches (6.4 cm) Neptune	.3 inches (.8 cm) Mars
A little over .5 inches (1.3 cm) Earth	.25 inches (.6 cm) Mercury

Take a look at your circles. Which planets are closest in size?
What do you think these planets have in common?

Fun Facts

- Jupiter is the heaviest planet in our solar system.

- Jupiter is very cold at the top of its atmosphere and very hot deep inside its core. The temperature high at the top of Jupiter's clouds is minus 230 degrees Fahrenheit (minus 146 degrees Celsius). The temperature at the core may be 43,000 F (23,890 C). That's hotter than the sun!

- Jupiter bulges at the middle and is slightly flattened at the poles.

- Jupiter is tilted on its axis only slightly. This means that the planet doesn't really have seasons. The amount of light it receives from the sun is about the same all year long.

- British scientist Robert Hooke may have been the first person to see Jupiter's Great Red Spot, in 1664.

Glossary

atmosphere—the gases that surround a planet

axis—the center on which something spins, or rotates

dense—having a lot of mass packed into a limited space

diameter—the distance of a line running from one side of a circle, through the center, and across to the other side

gravity—the force that pulls things down toward the surface of a planet

orbit—the path an object takes to travel around a star or planet; also, to travel around a star or planet

solar system—the sun and the bodies that orbit around it; these bodies include planets, moons, dwarf planets, asteroids, and comets

telescope—a device with mirrors or lenses; a telescope makes faraway objects appear closer

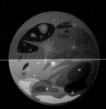

To Learn More

More Books to Read

Asimov, Isaac, with revisions and updating by Richard Hantula. *Jupiter*.
    Milwaukee: Gareth Stevens Pub., 2002.
Ring, Susan. *Jupiter*. New York: Weigl Publishers, 2004.
Simon, Charnan. *Jupiter*. Chanhassen, Minn.: Child's World, 2004.

On the Web

FactHound offers a safe, fun way to find Web sites related to topics in this book.
All of the sites on FactHound have been researched by our staff.

1. Visit *www.facthound.com*
2. Type in this special code: 1404839526
3. Click on the FETCH IT button.

Your trusty FactHound will fetch the best sites for you!

Index

Look for all of the books in the Amazing Science: Planets series:

Brightest in the Sky: The Planet Venus
Dwarf Planets: Pluto, Charon, Ceres, and Eris
Farthest from the Sun: The Planet Neptune
The Largest Planet: Jupiter
Nearest to the Sun: The Planet Mercury
Our Home Planet: Earth
Ringed Giant: The Planet Saturn
Seeing Red: The Planet Mars
The Sideways Planet: Uranus